Daily
Cash Flow Log Book

NAME: _____

PHONE: _____

ADDRESS: _____

DATE FROM:___/___/___   TO:___/___/___   PREV, BALANCE:_____

DATE	DESCRIPTION	CASH IN	CASH OUT	BALANCE
	TOTAL			

DATE: :___/___/___   SIGNED:

| DATE FROM:___/___/___ | | TO:___/___/___ | | PREV, BALANCE:_____ |

DATE	DESCRIPTION	CASH IN	CASH OUT	BALANCE
TOTAL				

| DATE: :___/___/___ | SIGNED: |

DATE FROM:___/___/___   TO:___/___/___   PREV, BALANCE:_____

DATE	DESCRIPTION	CASH IN	CASH OUT	BALANCE
TOTAL				

DATE: :___/___/___   SIGNED:

DATE FROM:___/___/___   TO:___/___/___   PREV, BALANCE:_____

DATE	DESCRIPTION	CASH IN	CASH OUT	BALANCE
	TOTAL			

DATE: :___/___/___   SIGNED:

DATE FROM:___/___/___   TO:___/___/___   PREV, BALANCE:_____

DATE	DESCRIPTION	CASH IN	CASH OUT	BALANCE
	TOTAL			

DATE: :___/___/___   SIGNED:

DATE FROM:___/___/___   TO:___/___/___   PREV, BALANCE:_____

DATE	DESCRIPTION	CASH IN	CASH OUT	BALANCE
	TOTAL			

DATE: :___/___/___   SIGNED:

DATE FROM:___/___/___   TO:___/___/___   PREV, BALANCE:_____

DATE	DESCRIPTION	CASH IN	CASH OUT	BALANCE
TOTAL				

DATE: :___/___/___   SIGNED:

DATE FROM:___/___/___	TO:___/___/___	PREV, BALANCE:_____

DATE	DESCRIPTION	CASH IN	CASH OUT	BALANCE
TOTAL				

DATE: :___/___/___	SIGNED:

DATE FROM:___/___/___   TO:___/___/___   PREV, BALANCE:_____

DATE	DESCRIPTION	CASH IN	CASH OUT	BALANCE
TOTAL				

DATE: :___/___/___   SIGNED:

DATE FROM:___/___/___   TO:___/___/___   PREV, BALANCE:_____

DATE	DESCRIPTION	CASH IN	CASH OUT	BALANCE
TOTAL				

DATE: :___/___/___   SIGNED:

DATE FROM:___/___/___   TO:___/___/___   PREV, BALANCE:_____

DATE	DESCRIPTION	CASH IN	CASH OUT	BALANCE
	TOTAL			

DATE: :___/___/___   SIGNED:

DATE FROM:___/___/___   TO:___/___/___   PREV, BALANCE:_____

DATE	DESCRIPTION	CASH IN	CASH OUT	BALANCE
	TOTAL			

DATE: :___/___/___   SIGNED:

DATE FROM:___/___/___   TO:___/___/___   PREV, BALANCE:_____

DATE	DESCRIPTION	CASH IN	CASH OUT	BALANCE
	TOTAL			

DATE: :___/___/___   SIGNED:

DATE FROM:___/___/___   TO:___/___/___   PREV, BALANCE:_____

DATE	DESCRIPTION	CASH IN	CASH OUT	BALANCE
	TOTAL			

DATE: :___/___/___   SIGNED:

DATE FROM:___/___/___   TO:___/___/___   PREV, BALANCE:_____

DATE	DESCRIPTION	CASH IN	CASH OUT	BALANCE
TOTAL				

DATE: :___/___/___   SIGNED:

DATE FROM:___/___/___   TO:___/___/___   PREV, BALANCE:_____

DATE	DESCRIPTION	CASH IN	CASH OUT	BALANCE
TOTAL				

DATE: :___/___/___   SIGNED:

DATE FROM:___/___/___   TO:___/___/___   PREV, BALANCE:_____

DATE	DESCRIPTION	CASH IN	CASH OUT	BALANCE
TOTAL				

DATE: :___/___/___   SIGNED:

DATE FROM:___/___/___   TO:___/___/___   PREV, BALANCE:_____

DATE	DESCRIPTION	CASH IN	CASH OUT	BALANCE
TOTAL				

DATE: :___/___/___   SIGNED:

DATE FROM:___/___/___   TO:___/___/___   PREV, BALANCE:_____

DATE	DESCRIPTION	CASH IN	CASH OUT	BALANCE
	TOTAL			

DATE: :___/___/___   SIGNED:

DATE FROM:___/___/___   TO:___/___/___   PREV, BALANCE:_____

DATE	DESCRIPTION	CASH IN	CASH OUT	BALANCE
TOTAL				

DATE: :___/___/___   SIGNED:

DATE FROM:___/___/___	TO:___/___/___	PREV, BALANCE:_____

DATE	DESCRIPTION	CASH IN	CASH OUT	BALANCE
TOTAL				

DATE: :___/___/___	SIGNED:

DATE FROM:___/___/___   TO:___/___/___   PREV, BALANCE:_____

DATE	DESCRIPTION	CASH IN	CASH OUT	BALANCE
TOTAL				

DATE: :___/___/___   SIGNED:

DATE FROM:___/___/___   TO:___/___/___   PREV, BALANCE:_____

DATE	DESCRIPTION	CASH IN	CASH OUT	BALANCE
TOTAL				

DATE: :___/___/___   SIGNED:

DATE FROM:___/___/___   TO:___/___/___   PREV, BALANCE:_____

DATE	DESCRIPTION	CASH IN	CASH OUT	BALANCE
	TOTAL			

DATE: :___/___/___   SIGNED:

DATE FROM:___/___/___   TO:___/___/___   PREV, BALANCE:_____

DATE	DESCRIPTION	CASH IN	CASH OUT	BALANCE
TOTAL				

DATE: :___/___/___   SIGNED:

DATE FROM:___/___/___   TO:___/___/___   PREV, BALANCE:_____

DATE	DESCRIPTION	CASH IN	CASH OUT	BALANCE
TOTAL				

DATE: :___/___/___   SIGNED:

DATE FROM:___/___/___   TO:___/___/___   PREV, BALANCE:_____

DATE	DESCRIPTION	CASH IN	CASH OUT	BALANCE
TOTAL				

DATE: :___/___/___   SIGNED:

DATE FROM:___/___/___   TO:___/___/___   PREV, BALANCE:_____

DATE	DESCRIPTION	CASH IN	CASH OUT	BALANCE
TOTAL				

DATE: :___/___/___   SIGNED:

DATE FROM:___/___/___   TO:___/___/___   PREV, BALANCE:_____

DATE	DESCRIPTION	CASH IN	CASH OUT	BALANCE
	TOTAL			

DATE: :___/___/___   SIGNED:

DATE FROM:___/___/___   TO:___/___/___   PREV, BALANCE:_____

DATE	DESCRIPTION	CASH IN	CASH OUT	BALANCE
	TOTAL			

DATE: :___/___/___   SIGNED:

DATE FROM:___/___/___   TO:___/___/___   PREV, BALANCE:_____

DATE	DESCRIPTION	CASH IN	CASH OUT	BALANCE
	TOTAL			

DATE: :___/___/___   SIGNED:

DATE FROM:___/___/___   TO:___/___/___   PREV, BALANCE:_____

DATE	DESCRIPTION	CASH IN	CASH OUT	BALANCE
	TOTAL			

DATE: :___/___/___   SIGNED:

DATE FROM:___/___/___   TO:___/___/___   PREV, BALANCE:_____

DATE	DESCRIPTION	CASH IN	CASH OUT	BALANCE
TOTAL				

DATE: :___/___/___   SIGNED:

DATE FROM:___/___/___   TO:___/___/___   PREV, BALANCE:_____

DATE	DESCRIPTION	CASH IN	CASH OUT	BALANCE
TOTAL				

DATE: :___/___/___   SIGNED:

DATE FROM:___/___/___   TO:___/___/___   PREV, BALANCE:_____

DATE	DESCRIPTION	CASH IN	CASH OUT	BALANCE
	TOTAL			

DATE: :___/___/___   SIGNED:

DATE FROM:___/___/___   TO:___/___/___   PREV, BALANCE:_____

DATE	DESCRIPTION	CASH IN	CASH OUT	BALANCE
TOTAL				

DATE: :___/___/___   SIGNED:

DATE FROM:___/___/___   TO:___/___/___   PREV, BALANCE:_____

DATE	DESCRIPTION	CASH IN	CASH OUT	BALANCE
TOTAL				

DATE: :___/___/___   SIGNED:

DATE FROM: ___ / ___ / ___   TO: ___ / ___ / ___   PREV, BALANCE: _____

DATE	DESCRIPTION	CASH IN	CASH OUT	BALANCE
	TOTAL			

DATE: : ___ / ___ / ___   SIGNED:

DATE FROM:___/___/___   TO:___/___/___   PREV, BALANCE:_____

DATE	DESCRIPTION	CASH IN	CASH OUT	BALANCE
TOTAL				

DATE: :___/___/___   SIGNED:

DATE FROM:___/___/___   TO:___/___/___   PREV, BALANCE:_____

DATE	DESCRIPTION	CASH IN	CASH OUT	BALANCE
TOTAL				

DATE: :___/___/___   SIGNED:

DATE FROM: ___/___/___   TO:___/___/___   PREV, BALANCE:_____

DATE	DESCRIPTION	CASH IN	CASH OUT	BALANCE
TOTAL				

DATE: :___/___/___   SIGNED:

DATE FROM:___/___/___	TO:___/___/___	PREV, BALANCE:_____

DATE	DESCRIPTION	CASH IN	CASH OUT	BALANCE
TOTAL				

DATE: :___/___/___	SIGNED:

DATE FROM:___/___/___   TO:___/___/___   PREV, BALANCE:_____

DATE	DESCRIPTION	CASH IN	CASH OUT	BALANCE
	TOTAL			

DATE: :___/___/___   SIGNED:

DATE FROM:___/___/___   TO:___/___/___   PREV, BALANCE:_____

DATE	DESCRIPTION	CASH IN	CASH OUT	BALANCE
TOTAL				

DATE : :___/___/___   SIGNED:

DATE FROM:___/___/___   TO:___/___/___   PREV, BALANCE:_____

DATE	DESCRIPTION	CASH IN	CASH OUT	BALANCE
TOTAL				

DATE: :___/___/___   SIGNED:

DATE FROM:__/__/__   TO:___/___/___   PREV, BALANCE:_____

DATE	DESCRIPTION	CASH IN	CASH OUT	BALANCE
	TOTAL			

DATE: :__/__/__   SIGNED:

DATE FROM:___/___/___   TO:___/___/___   PREV, BALANCE:_____

DATE	DESCRIPTION	CASH IN	CASH OUT	BALANCE
TOTAL				

DATE: :___/___/___   SIGNED:

DATE FROM:___/___/___   TO:___/___/___   PREV, BALANCE:_____

DATE	DESCRIPTION	CASH IN	CASH OUT	BALANCE
TOTAL				

DATE: :___/___/___   SIGNED:

DATE FROM:___/___/___   TO:___/___/___   PREV, BALANCE:_____

DATE	DESCRIPTION	CASH IN	CASH OUT	BALANCE
	TOTAL			

DATE: :___/___/___   SIGNED:

DATE FROM: ___/___/___   TO:___/___/___   PREV, BALANCE:_____

DATE	DESCRIPTION	CASH IN	CASH OUT	BALANCE
TOTAL				

DATE: :___/___/___   SIGNED:

DATE FROM: ___/___/___   TO:___/___/___   PREV, BALANCE:_____

DATE	DESCRIPTION	CASH IN	CASH OUT	BALANCE
	TOTAL			

DATE: :___/___/___   SIGNED:

DATE FROM:___/___/___   TO:___/___/___   PREV, BALANCE:_____

DATE	DESCRIPTION	CASH IN	CASH OUT	BALANCE
TOTAL				

DATE: :___/___/___   SIGNED:

DATE FROM:___/___/___   TO:___/___/___   PREV, BALANCE:_____

DATE	DESCRIPTION	CASH IN	CASH OUT	BALANCE
	TOTAL			

DATE: :___/___/___   SIGNED:

DATE FROM:___/___/___   TO:___/___/___   PREV, BALANCE:_____

DATE	DESCRIPTION	CASH IN	CASH OUT	BALANCE
TOTAL				

DATE: :___/___/___   SIGNED:

DATE FROM:___/___/___   TO:___/___/___   PREV, BALANCE:_____

DATE	DESCRIPTION	CASH IN	CASH OUT	BALANCE
TOTAL				

DATE: :___/___/___   SIGNED:

DATE FROM:___/___/___   TO:___/___/___   PREV, BALANCE:_____

DATE	DESCRIPTION	CASH IN	CASH OUT	BALANCE
	TOTAL			

DATE: :___/___/___   SIGNED:

DATE FROM:___/___/___   TO:___/___/___   PREV, BALANCE:_____

DATE	DESCRIPTION	CASH IN	CASH OUT	BALANCE
TOTAL				

DATE: :___/___/___   SIGNED:

DATE FROM:___/___/___   TO:___/___/___   PREV, BALANCE:_____

DATE	DESCRIPTION	CASH IN	CASH OUT	BALANCE
	TOTAL			

DATE: :___/___/___   SIGNED:

DATE FROM:___/___/___   TO:___/___/___   PREV, BALANCE:_____

DATE	DESCRIPTION	CASH IN	CASH OUT	BALANCE
TOTAL				

DATE: :___/___/___   SIGNED:

DATE FROM:___/___/___   TO:___/___/___   PREV, BALANCE:_____

DATE	DESCRIPTION	CASH IN	CASH OUT	BALANCE
TOTAL				

DATE: :___/___/___   SIGNED:

DATE FROM:___/___/___   TO:___/___/___   PREV, BALANCE:_____

DATE	DESCRIPTION	CASH IN	CASH OUT	BALANCE
TOTAL				

DATE: :___/___/___   SIGNED:

DATE FROM:___/___/___   TO:___/___/___   PREV, BALANCE:_____

DATE	DESCRIPTION	CASH IN	CASH OUT	BALANCE
TOTAL				

DATE: :___/___/___   SIGNED:

DATE FROM:___/___/___   TO:___/___/___   PREV, BALANCE:_____

DATE	DESCRIPTION	CASH IN	CASH OUT	BALANCE
TOTAL				

DATE: :___/___/___   SIGNED:

DATE FROM:___/___/___   TO:___/___/___   PREV, BALANCE:_____

DATE	DESCRIPTION	CASH IN	CASH OUT	BALANCE
	TOTAL			

DATE: :___/___/___   SIGNED:

DATE FROM:___/___/___   TO:___/___/___   PREV, BALANCE:_____

DATE	DESCRIPTION	CASH IN	CASH OUT	BALANCE
TOTAL				

DATE: :___/___/___   SIGNED:

DATE FROM:___/___/___   TO:___/___/___   PREV, BALANCE:_____

DATE	DESCRIPTION	CASH IN	CASH OUT	BALANCE
TOTAL				

DATE: :___/___/___   SIGNED:

DATE FROM:___/___/___   TO:___/___/___   PREV, BALANCE:_____

DATE	DESCRIPTION	CASH IN	CASH OUT	BALANCE
TOTAL				

DATE: :___/___/___   SIGNED:

DATE FROM:___/___/___   TO:___/___/___   PREV, BALANCE:_____

DATE	DESCRIPTION	CASH IN	CASH OUT	BALANCE
TOTAL				

DATE: :___/___/___   SIGNED:

DATE FROM:___/___/___   TO:___/___/___   PREV, BALANCE:_____

DATE	DESCRIPTION	CASH IN	CASH OUT	BALANCE
TOTAL				

DATE: :___/___/___   SIGNED:

DATE FROM:___/___/___   TO:___/___/___   PREV, BALANCE:_____

DATE	DESCRIPTION	CASH IN	CASH OUT	BALANCE
	TOTAL			

DATE: :___/___/___   SIGNED:

DATE FROM:___/___/___   TO:___/___/___   PREV, BALANCE:_____

DATE	DESCRIPTION	CASH IN	CASH OUT	BALANCE
	TOTAL			

DATE: :___/___/___   SIGNED:

DATE FROM:___/___/___   TO:___/___/___   PREV, BALANCE:_____

DATE	DESCRIPTION	CASH IN	CASH OUT	BALANCE
TOTAL				

DATE: :___/___/___   SIGNED:

DATE FROM:___/___/___   TO:___/___/___   PREV, BALANCE:_____

DATE	DESCRIPTION	CASH IN	CASH OUT	BALANCE
TOTAL				

DATE: :___/___/___   SIGNED:

DATE FROM:___/___/___   TO:___/___/___   PREV, BALANCE:_____

DATE	DESCRIPTION	CASH IN	CASH OUT	BALANCE
TOTAL				

DATE: :___/___/___   SIGNED:

DATE FROM:___/___/___   TO:___/___/___   PREV, BALANCE:_____

DATE	DESCRIPTION	CASH IN	CASH OUT	BALANCE
TOTAL				

DATE: :___/___/___   SIGNED:

DATE FROM:___/___/___   TO:___/___/___   PREV, BALANCE:_____

DATE	DESCRIPTION	CASH IN	CASH OUT	BALANCE
	TOTAL			

DATE: :___/___/___   SIGNED:

DATE FROM:___/___/___   TO:___/___/___   PREV, BALANCE:_____

DATE	DESCRIPTION	CASH IN	CASH OUT	BALANCE
TOTAL				

DATE: :___/___/___   SIGNED:

DATE FROM:___/___/___   TO:___/___/___   PREV, BALANCE:_____

DATE	DESCRIPTION	CASH IN	CASH OUT	BALANCE
TOTAL				

DATE: :___/___/___   SIGNED:

DATE FROM:___/___/___   TO:___/___/___   PREV, BALANCE:_____

DATE	DESCRIPTION	CASH IN	CASH OUT	BALANCE
TOTAL				

DATE: :___/___/___   SIGNED:

DATE FROM:___/___/___   TO:___/___/___   PREV, BALANCE:_____

DATE	DESCRIPTION	CASH IN	CASH OUT	BALANCE
TOTAL				

DATE: :___/___/___   SIGNED:

DATE FROM:___/___/___   TO:___/___/___   PREV, BALANCE:_____

DATE	DESCRIPTION	CASH IN	CASH OUT	BALANCE
TOTAL				

DATE: :___/___/___   SIGNED:

DATE FROM:___/___/___   TO:___/___/___   PREV, BALANCE:_____

DATE	DESCRIPTION	CASH IN	CASH OUT	BALANCE
TOTAL				

DATE: :___/___/___   SIGNED:

DATE FROM:___/___/___   TO:___/___/___   PREV, BALANCE:_____

DATE	DESCRIPTION	CASH IN	CASH OUT	BALANCE
TOTAL				

DATE: :___/___/___   SIGNED:

DATE FROM:___/___/___   TO:___/___/___   PREV, BALANCE:_____

DATE	DESCRIPTION	CASH IN	CASH OUT	BALANCE
TOTAL				

DATE: :___/___/___   SIGNED:

DATE FROM:___/___/___   TO:___/___/___   PREV, BALANCE:_____

DATE	DESCRIPTION	CASH IN	CASH OUT	BALANCE
TOTAL				

DATE: :___/___/___   SIGNED:

DATE FROM:___/___/___   TO:___/___/___   PREV, BALANCE:_____

DATE	DESCRIPTION	CASH IN	CASH OUT	BALANCE
	TOTAL			

DATE: :___/___/___   SIGNED:

DATE FROM:___/___/___   TO:___/___/___   PREV, BALANCE:_____

DATE	DESCRIPTION	CASH IN	CASH OUT	BALANCE
TOTAL				

DATE: :___/___/___   SIGNED:

DATE FROM:___/___/___   TO:___/___/___   PREV, BALANCE:_____

DATE	DESCRIPTION	CASH IN	CASH OUT	BALANCE
TOTAL				

DATE: ___/___/___   SIGNED:

DATE FROM:___/___/___   TO:___/___/___   PREV, BALANCE:_____

DATE	DESCRIPTION	CASH IN	CASH OUT	BALANCE
TOTAL				

DATE: :___/___/___   SIGNED:

DATE FROM:___/___/___   TO:___/___/___   PREV, BALANCE:_____

DATE	DESCRIPTION	CASH IN	CASH OUT	BALANCE
TOTAL				

DATE: :___/___/___   SIGNED:

DATE FROM:___/___/___   TO:___/___/___   PREV, BALANCE:_____

DATE	DESCRIPTION	CASH IN	CASH OUT	BALANCE
TOTAL				

DATE :___/___/___   SIGNED:

DATE FROM:___/___/___   TO:___/___/___   PREV, BALANCE:_____

DATE	DESCRIPTION	CASH IN	CASH OUT	BALANCE
	TOTAL			

DATE: :___/___/___   SIGNED:

DATE FROM:___/___/___   TO:___/___/___   PREV, BALANCE:_____

DATE	DESCRIPTION	CASH IN	CASH OUT	BALANCE
	TOTAL			

DATE: :___/___/___   SIGNED:

DATE FROM:___/___/___   TO:___/___/___   PREV, BALANCE:_____

DATE	DESCRIPTION	CASH IN	CASH OUT	BALANCE
TOTAL				

DATE: :___/___/___   SIGNED:

DATE FROM:___/___/___   TO:___/___/___   PREV, BALANCE:_____

DATE	DESCRIPTION	CASH IN	CASH OUT	BALANCE
TOTAL				

DATE: :___/___/___   SIGNED:

DATE FROM:___/___/___   TO:___/___/___   PREV, BALANCE:_____

DATE	DESCRIPTION	CASH IN	CASH OUT	BALANCE
TOTAL				

DATE: ___/___/___   SIGNED:

DATE FROM:___/___/___   TO:___/___/___   PREV, BALANCE:_____

DATE	DESCRIPTION	CASH IN	CASH OUT	BALANCE
	TOTAL			

DATE: :___/___/___   SIGNED:

DATE FROM:___/___/___   TO:___/___/___   PREV, BALANCE:_____

DATE	DESCRIPTION	CASH IN	CASH OUT	BALANCE
TOTAL				

DATE: :___/___/___   SIGNED:

DATE FROM:___/___/___   TO:___/___/___   PREV, BALANCE:_____

DATE	DESCRIPTION	CASH IN	CASH OUT	BALANCE
TOTAL				

DATE: :___/___/___   SIGNED:

DATE FROM:___/___/___   TO:___/___/___   PREV, BALANCE:_____

DATE	DESCRIPTION	CASH IN	CASH OUT	BALANCE
	TOTAL			

DATE: :___/___/___   SIGNED:

DATE FROM:___/___/___   TO:___/___/___   PREV, BALANCE:_____

DATE	DESCRIPTION	CASH IN	CASH OUT	BALANCE
TOTAL				

DATE: :___/___/___   SIGNED:

DATE FROM:___/___/___   TO:___/___/___   PREV, BALANCE:_____

DATE	DESCRIPTION	CASH IN	CASH OUT	BALANCE
	TOTAL			

DATE: :___/___/___   SIGNED:

DATE FROM:___/___/___   TO:___/___/___   PREV, BALANCE:_____

DATE	DESCRIPTION	CASH IN	CASH OUT	BALANCE
TOTAL				

DATE: :___/___/___   SIGNED:

DATE FROM:___/___/___   TO:___/___/___   PREV, BALANCE:_____

DATE	DESCRIPTION	CASH IN	CASH OUT	BALANCE
TOTAL				

DATE: :___/___/___   SIGNED:

DATE FROM:___/___/___   TO:___/___/___   PREV, BALANCE:_____

DATE	DESCRIPTION	CASH IN	CASH OUT	BALANCE
TOTAL				

DATE: :___/___/___   SIGNED:

DATE FROM:___/___/___   TO:___/___/___   PREV, BALANCE:_____

DATE	DESCRIPTION	CASH IN	CASH OUT	BALANCE
	TOTAL			

DATE: :___/___/___   SIGNED:

DATE FROM:___/___/___   TO:___/___/___   PREV, BALANCE:_____

DATE	DESCRIPTION	CASH IN	CASH OUT	BALANCE
TOTAL				

DATE: :___/___/___   SIGNED:

Made in the USA
Middletown, DE
24 October 2023